The 12 Days of Minimalist Christmas

A minimalism coffee table book for those wanting to declutter before christmas

Clara Brooks

Contents

Introduction - Rediscovering Christmas	v
1. Day 1: Clearing the Calendar	1
2. Day 2: Declutter Décor	4
3. Day 3 – Rethink Gifts	7
4. Day 4 – Simplify Wrapping and Packaging	10
5. Day 5 – Declutter Digitally	13
6. Day 6 – Minimalist Meal Planning	16
7. Day 7 – A Minimalist Approach with Kids	19
8. Day 8 – Streamline Social Obligations	22
9. Day 9 – Financial Mindfulness	25
10. Day 10 – Acts of Kindness and Community	28
11. Day 11 – Crafting Meaningful Traditions	31
12. Day 12 – A Mindful Christmas Day	34
13. Appendix – Minimalist Christmas Checklist	37
Conclusion – Carrying Minimalism Forward	41
Author's Note	43

Introduction - Rediscovering Christmas

For many of us, Christmas arrives with a mix of excitement and exhaustion. We look forward to the lights, the food, the music, and the togetherness. At the same time, we feel the pressure to make it all "perfect." The season that was meant to be joyful often leaves us stressed, overspent, and surrounded by clutter we neither need nor have room for.

> "We wish for peace, yet fill our calendars. We crave connection, yet buy distraction."

Surveys show this is not just a personal feeling. It is a widespread reality. In one recent national poll, **90% of people said they wished the holidays were less materialistic** and 87% believed the season should be more about family and caring for others than gift-giving. These are not the complaints of Scrooges or Grinches. They are the voices of people longing for a holiday that feels more human, more present, and more connected.

Introduction - Rediscovering Christmas

What is a Minimalist Christmas?

A *Minimalist Christmas* is not about stripping away everything that makes the season special. It is not about living in a bare apartment with a single sprig of holly or refusing to give gifts altogether unless that is what truly feels right to you.

Instead, it is about:

- **Less clutter** in your home, mind, and schedule.
- **More presence** by focusing on experiences and relationships instead of possessions.
- **Mindful consumption** that does not drain your wallet, your energy, or the planet's resources.
- **Space for meaning** by creating moments that nourish rather than deplete.

> **Key Idea:** *Minimalism is not the absence of celebration. It is the presence of what matters most.*

It is a conscious rejection of the "more is better" holiday formula we have been sold. Instead, it asks: *What if doing less actually gave you more?*

How Commercial Excess Has Distorted Holiday Joy

For decades, the holiday season has been framed as a shopping season first and a time of connection second. Advertisements start earlier each year. Black Friday turns into Cyber Week and then into a month of sales. Social media showcases meticulously styled homes and lavish piles of gifts under the tree, and we feel the pull to keep up.

The cost is high:

- Families going into debt for gifts forgotten by February.
- Parents spending December in shops instead of making memories at home.
- Homes overflowing with seasonal décor that is used once and then stored or discarded.

Introduction - Rediscovering Christmas

• Calendars so packed that we cannot pause long enough to enjoy the season.

Key Idea: *Every "yes" to something that does not matter is a "no" to something that does.*

Minimalism offers a different path. It invites us to step away from the conveyor belt of consumption and choose a slower and more intentional celebration that gives us permission to breathe.

What This Book Will Give You

The 12 Days of Minimalist Christmas is a practical and inspiring guide to help you reclaim the holidays from chaos and consumerism. Each of the **12 chapters** focuses on a specific aspect of simplification such as clearing your calendar, rethinking gifts, reducing waste, and creating new traditions.

How to Use This Book:

• **Daily Focus** – Each "day" offers one theme so you can make manageable changes without feeling overwhelmed.

• **Action Steps** – Practical and realistic tips you can apply immediately.

• **Reflection Prompts** – Gentle questions to help you define what truly matters to you this season.

• **Global Inspiration** – Ideas drawn from traditions around the world that celebrate connection instead of consumerism.

You can read the book straight through or dip into the chapters that speak to your most pressing holiday challenges. Whether you start in mid-December or months before, these steps will help you design a holiday season that is lighter, calmer, and more joyful.

"The spirit of Christmas does not come wrapped in shiny paper. It is found in the moments we slow down enough to see it."

Introduction - Rediscovering Christmas

This is not about doing Christmas "the minimalist way" because someone else says so. It is about discovering *your* way. It is about walking into the New Year with a full heart instead of an empty wallet and a cluttered home.

Chapter 1
Day 1: Clearing the Calendar

One of the easiest ways to simplify Christmas is to start with your time. In many households, the December calendar fills up before we have a chance to think. Parties, school plays, charity events, shopping trips, and extended family gatherings all seem important. The result is a month that feels more like a marathon than a celebration.

The first step toward a minimalist Christmas is to look at your schedule with intention. Instead of accepting every invitation, pause and ask yourself: *Does this bring me joy? Does this align with my values for the season?* If the answer is no, you are allowed to decline.

Why a Clear Calendar Matters

Time is one of your most precious resources. Once it is gone, you cannot get it back. A crowded calendar often leads to exhaustion, stress, and resentment. It leaves little room for the quiet moments that make Christmas meaningful, such as reading by the tree, enjoying a simple dinner with family, or taking a peaceful evening walk to admire the lights.

Clara Brooks

Key Idea: *When you say yes to everything, you end up saying no to what matters most.*

By choosing fewer commitments, you give yourself and your loved ones the gift of space. That space allows for rest, presence, and deeper connection.

How to Clear Your Holiday Calendar

1 List everything you are committed to

Write down all events, obligations, and traditions you expect to take part in this December.

2 Identify the essentials

Circle the events that genuinely bring you joy or fulfill an important purpose. These stay.

3 Let go of the rest

For the events that are not essential, decide whether you can decline, delegate, or scale back.

4 Practice saying no with grace

You do not need a long explanation. A simple "Thank you for the invitation, but I am keeping things simple this year" is enough.

5 Protect open days

Treat unscheduled time as valuable. These are opportunities for spontaneous fun or quiet rest.

Reflection Prompt

Think about the last holiday season. Which events left you feeling warm and fulfilled? Which ones drained your energy? Use your answers to guide your choices this year.

The 12 Days of Minimalist Christmas

By starting with your calendar, you set the tone for the rest of your minimalist Christmas journey. The goal is not to do nothing, but to choose wisely so that each activity has space to be enjoyed.

Chapter 2
Day 2: Declutter Décor

For many households, holiday decorations take up more space than any other seasonal tradition. Boxes of ornaments, wreaths, lights, figurines, and novelty items fill attics and closets, only to be unpacked for a few weeks each year. While decorations can be fun, they can also create clutter, stress, and unnecessary expense.

Minimalist décor is not about removing all festive touches. It is about choosing a few meaningful items and letting them shine. The goal is to create an atmosphere of warmth and beauty without overwhelming your home or your budget.

Why Simplify Your Decorations?

When we decorate mindlessly, the result is often excess. We buy more than we need, fill our spaces until they feel crowded, and then struggle to store everything when the season ends. Decorations that once sparked joy can start to feel like obligations.

The 12 Days of Minimalist Christmas

Key Idea: *More décor does not equal more cheer.*

Simplifying your decorations frees space in your home, reduces waste, and lowers the pressure to keep up with consumer trends. It also makes set-up and clean-up quicker, giving you more time to enjoy the season.

How to Declutter Décor

1 Take everything out

Unpack your holiday boxes and lay out every item where you can see it.

2 Sort with intention

Keep what is truly meaningful or beautiful. Donate or recycle the rest.

3 Choose a theme or color palette

A simple theme makes decorating easier and more cohesive. It also prevents impulse purchases.

4 Embrace natural materials

Pinecones, evergreen branches, oranges, or eucalyptus can add beauty and can be composted afterward.

5 Limit storage

Decide how many boxes or bins you want to dedicate to holiday décor. This boundary keeps clutter from creeping back in.

Alternative Decorating Ideas

- Create a centerpiece with candles and greenery instead of covering every surface.
- Hang a single wreath or string of lights instead of multiple large displays.
- Consider a smaller or alternative tree such as a potted plant, a branch in a vase, or a reused artificial tree made of recycled materials.

. . .

Reflection Prompt

Look at your decorations and ask: *Which items truly spark joy and carry meaning? Which ones do I keep out of habit or obligation?*

Decluttering your décor sets the stage for a calmer and more intentional holiday season. A few thoughtful touches can create just as much magic as a house full of objects, while leaving your home open, breathable, and easy to enjoy.

Chapter 3
Day 3 – Rethink Gifts

Gift giving is one of the most joyful parts of Christmas, but it is also one of the most stressful. Every year people feel pressure to buy more, spend more, and find the "perfect" item. The result is often financial strain, clutter, and disappointment when gifts are forgotten or unused.

A minimalist approach does not mean refusing to give. It means giving with intention. The focus shifts from piles of packages to thoughtful choices that express care without creating excess.

Why Rethink Gift Giving?

Statistics show that billions are spent each holiday season on gifts that go unused or are returned. Many families also carry holiday debt into the new year. Beyond money, there is the emotional weight of shopping trips, wrapping marathons, and the silent competition to "keep up" with others.

Clara Brooks

Key Idea: *Gifts should add meaning, not stress.*

By rethinking gift giving, you can replace obligation with creativity and waste with value.

Minimalist Gift Approaches
1 The Four Gift Rule
For children, some families use this simple guide: something they want, something they need, something to wear, and something to read.

2 Experiences over things
Consider tickets to a show, a day trip, or a cooking class. Experiences create memories that last longer than objects.

3 Secondhand and handmade gifts
The stigma around giving secondhand is fading. Beautiful books, toys, or vintage items can be treasures. Handmade gifts such as baked goods, art, or crafted items carry a personal touch.

4 Consumables
Food, candles, or bath products are enjoyed and then gone, leaving no clutter behind.

5 Charitable giving
Donate to a cause in someone's name. This is especially powerful for recipients who value generosity more than possessions.

How to Set Boundaries Around Gifts
- **Have honest conversations** with family and friends. Many people will feel relief when someone suggests reducing the gift exchange.
- **Agree on limits** such as drawing names, setting price caps, or choosing experiences instead of physical items.
- **Be polite but firm** if others insist on giving more. A gracious

The 12 Days of Minimalist Christmas

"Thank you, but please know we are keeping things simple this year" can set the tone.

Reflection Prompt

Think about the most meaningful gift you have ever received. What made it special? Was it the cost, or was it the thought and connection behind it?

By rethinking gifts, you shift Christmas from a season of shopping to a season of sharing. Each present becomes a symbol of love and care, not a burden on your budget or your space.

Chapter 4
Day 4 – Simplify Wrapping and Packaging

Wrapping paper, ribbons, bows, and tags are often treated as part of the magic of Christmas. Yet much of it is used once and thrown away. Glittery paper cannot be recycled, plastic bows end up in landfills, and miles of ribbon are wasted every December.

Simplifying your wrapping does not take away from the beauty of a gift. In fact, it can make presents feel more thoughtful. When you choose simple and sustainable methods, you create packages that look elegant, reduce waste, and save both time and money.

Why Wrapping Needs a Rethink

The holidays produce more household waste than any other time of year. Wrapping materials contribute significantly to that. If every family reused just a small portion of their wrapping supplies, the environmental impact would be enormous.

The 12 Days of Minimalist Christmas

Key Idea: *The outside of a gift should not cost more than the joy it holds inside.*

By simplifying your approach, you reduce clutter, avoid unnecessary purchases, and show that beauty can be found in simplicity.

Minimalist Wrapping Ideas

1 Reusable fabric

Try cloth wraps or scarves. The Japanese art of furoshiki turns fabric into a beautiful and waste-free wrapping option.

2 Recycled paper

Use brown kraft paper, newspaper, or old maps. Tie with string or twine for a rustic look.

3 Gift bags and boxes

Choose sturdy ones that can be reused year after year.

4 Natural accents

Decorate with sprigs of pine, dried orange slices, or cinnamon sticks instead of plastic bows.

5 Minimal tags

A handwritten note or a small piece of recycled card is often all you need.

Create a Wrapping Capsule

Keep a small collection of wrapping supplies that are versatile and reusable. A box of plain paper, fabric squares, string, and a few natural accents is enough for any occasion. This eliminates the need to buy new rolls of themed paper every season.

Reflection Prompt

Think about the last pile of wrapping paper you threw away. How could you have wrapped those gifts differently to avoid so much waste?

* * *

By simplifying your wrapping and packaging, you give yourself and others a gift that lasts beyond the season: less waste, less clutter, and a more mindful approach to beauty.

Chapter 5
Day 5 – Declutter Digitally

The clutter of Christmas is not only in our homes. It also shows up in our digital lives. Emails filled with holiday sales, endless notifications, and the constant scroll of social media can leave us feeling scattered and distracted. A minimalist Christmas also means creating peace in your digital space.

Digital clutter steals time and attention. Instead of being fully present with loved ones, we find ourselves checking messages, browsing deals, or comparing our holiday to someone else's perfect online version. Choosing to simplify your digital habits can free your mind and help you reconnect with the moments that matter.

Why Digital Decluttering Matters

The pressure of Christmas consumerism is amplified online. Advertisers flood inboxes and social feeds with offers. Friends post highlight reels that make us feel we are not doing enough. The result is stress and distraction during a time that should feel meaningful.

Key Idea: *Being present is the greatest gift you can give your loved ones.*

By taking control of your digital life, you remove constant noise and create more space for connection and rest.

How to Declutter Digitally

1 Unsubscribe from marketing emails

Spend ten minutes clearing out mailing lists that push endless holiday sales.

2 Clean your inbox

Archive or delete messages you no longer need. Create folders for the few that matter.

3 Set phone boundaries

Decide specific times to check messages instead of constantly picking up your phone.

4 Limit social media

Consider taking a short break, or log in only once a day. Remember that what you see online is not the whole story.

5 Tidy your devices

Remove unused apps, organize photos, and delete duplicates. Start the new year with a clean slate.

Create Device-Free Moments

Make certain times of day sacred. For example, Christmas Eve dinner, Christmas morning gift opening, or a family movie night can be marked as device-free zones. This encourages conversation, eye contact, and shared joy.

The 12 Days of Minimalist Christmas

Reflection Prompt

How much time did you spend last year scrolling during the holidays? What would you like to do with that time instead this year?

A digitally decluttered holiday feels calmer and more intentional. By putting your phone down and clearing your online space, you give yourself permission to live in the moment and experience Christmas with clarity and joy.

Chapter 6
Day 6 – Minimalist Meal Planning

Food is at the heart of Christmas. Tables are filled with roasts, side dishes, desserts, and drinks. The kitchen becomes a place of warmth and gathering. Yet for many families, holiday meals also bring stress, excess, and waste. Endless shopping lists, crowded fridges, and hours of preparation can take the joy out of sharing a meal.

Minimalist meal planning focuses on nourishment, togetherness, and simplicity. Instead of trying to cook everything, you choose a few dishes that matter most. You let go of the rest.

Why Simplify Holiday Meals?

Complicated meals take time, energy, and money. They often result in leftovers that go uneaten or food that ends up in the bin. Preparing too much also means less time for the people at the table.

Key Idea: *A meal shared with love is more memorable than a menu filled with excess.*

The 12 Days of Minimalist Christmas

Simplifying your meals ensures you enjoy both the cooking and the eating without being consumed by the process.

Steps to Minimalist Meal Planning

1 Choose your essentials

Decide which dishes truly make the holiday special. Keep those and let go of the rest.

2 Plan portions wisely

Prepare what your group will realistically eat. Avoid doubling recipes unless you know leftovers will be enjoyed.

3 Delegate and share

Invite guests to bring a side dish, dessert, or drink. Sharing the work creates connection and lightens your load.

4 Cook ahead where possible

Make soups, casseroles, or desserts the day before to reduce stress on the main day.

5 Use simple ingredients

Fresh, seasonal foods often taste best without too much complexity.

Alternative Meal Ideas

- Host a potluck dinner where everyone contributes one favorite dish.
- Try a theme such as "cozy comfort food" instead of a traditional feast.
- Replace one large meal with smaller shared plates that encourage conversation.

Reflection Prompt

What meals from past holidays do you remember most? Were they elaborate dishes or simple favorites enjoyed in good company?

Clara Brooks

* * *

Minimalist meal planning turns the focus away from a performance in the kitchen and back to the people around the table. The food becomes a backdrop for laughter, gratitude, and connection. That is the true flavor of Christmas.

Chapter 7
Day 7 – A Minimalist Approach with Kids

For parents, Christmas can feel like a balancing act. You want your children to feel the magic of the season, but you also want to avoid overwhelming them with toys, sugar, and nonstop activities. Advertisements and peer pressure can make it seem like "more" is always better, but children do not need mountains of gifts to feel loved.

A minimalist approach with kids is about teaching them that joy comes from experiences, connection, and gratitude. It is about creating traditions they will remember long after the toys are forgotten.

Why Less Is Better for Children

Studies show that too many toys can actually overwhelm children. They play less creatively when they are surrounded by excess. Piles of gifts can also set expectations that grow larger every year.

> **Key Idea:** *Children remember how they felt more than what they unwrapped.*

By offering fewer, more meaningful gifts and focusing on shared experiences, you give your children something richer than clutter.

Practical Ways to Simplify with Kids
1 Set gift limits
Use the Four Gift Rule (want, need, wear, read) or choose another simple system that works for your family.
2 Create experiences
Plan a baking day, a movie night, or a nature walk. These activities cost little but create lasting memories.
3 Teach generosity
Involve children in choosing a toy or book to donate. Let them experience the joy of giving to others.
4 Choose quality over quantity
Select gifts that encourage imagination, learning, or creativity instead of toys that will quickly be forgotten.
5 Simplify traditions
Pick a few activities your children love and repeat them each year. Consistency is more meaningful than a long checklist.

Family Activities Beyond Gifts
- Make handmade ornaments together.
- Start a Christmas Eve story-reading tradition.
- Create a "gratitude jar" where everyone adds notes about what they are thankful for.

Reflection Prompt
Think back to your own childhood. What stands out most from your Christmas memories? Was it the number of gifts, or was it the special traditions and the people around you?

The 12 Days of Minimalist Christmas

A minimalist approach with kids is not about denying them joy. It is about giving them a deeper sense of wonder, teaching them values that will last, and creating a holiday season that fills their hearts rather than their toy boxes.

Chapter 8
Day 8 – Streamline Social Obligations

The holiday season often brings a flood of invitations. Work parties, neighborhood gatherings, family dinners, community events, and school performances can quickly fill every evening in December. Many of these occasions are enjoyable, but too many can leave you drained.

Minimalism reminds us that we do not need to attend everything to have a meaningful Christmas. By choosing the gatherings that align with your values and gently declining the rest, you create space for rest and genuine connection.

Why It Helps to Simplify Your Social Calendar

When your calendar is packed, every event feels like an obligation rather than a joy. Rushing from place to place can leave little energy for the moments you truly want to savor.

Key Idea: *The best memories are made when you are present, not when you are rushing.*

The 12 Days of Minimalist Christmas

By streamlining your social commitments, you can show up with more energy and focus for the events that truly matter.

Steps to Streamline Your Social Life

1 Prioritize

Decide which events hold the most meaning for you and your family. Keep those.

2 Decline with kindness

A polite "Thank you for inviting me, but I will not be able to make it this year" is enough.

3 Limit hosting

If hosting creates stress, consider smaller gatherings or alternate years with friends and family.

4 Combine traditions

Merge social activities when possible, such as inviting friends to join your family's cookie-baking night instead of attending two separate events.

5 Leave early if needed

You do not need to stay until the very end. Attending briefly can still show support without exhausting yourself.

Ideas for Minimalist-Friendly Gatherings

- Host a simple potluck instead of a lavish dinner.
- Plan a walk to see neighborhood lights together.
- Share a board game night with warm drinks instead of a large party.

Reflection Prompt

Which gatherings bring you energy and joy, and which ones leave you feeling tired or stressed? How would your December look if you only attended the first group?

Clara Brooks

By streamlining your social obligations, you gain time for the activities and people who mean the most. Christmas becomes less about keeping up appearances and more about authentic connection.

Chapter 9
Day 9 – Financial Mindfulness

Money pressures often sit quietly beneath the surface of the holiday season. We want to be generous, to show love, and to create joy for others. Yet many people end up overspending, taking on debt, or feeling anxious as January bills arrive.

A minimalist Christmas invites you to approach finances with clarity. Instead of asking "How much should I spend?" you ask "What is truly enough?"

Why Money Matters in a Minimalist Christmas

Financial stress can overshadow even the happiest gatherings. When the season ends with regret or debt, the joy quickly fades. Choosing to spend mindfully allows you to give freely without damaging your peace of mind.

> **Key Idea:** *A gift given with love is never measured by its price.*

When you focus on meaning rather than money, you reduce stress and build healthier habits for years to come.

Steps to Practice Financial Mindfulness
1 Set a holiday budget early
Decide what you can comfortably spend before shopping begins. Write it down and stick to it.
2 Track your spending
Keep a simple list of every purchase. Awareness prevents small costs from adding up unnoticed.
3 Agree on limits with family
Suggest drawing names, setting a price cap, or skipping adult exchanges. Many will welcome the change.
4 Plan for experiences instead of things
Memories often cost less and mean more than material items.
5 Save for causes you care about
Redirect a portion of your holiday spending toward charity or community support. This brings deeper satisfaction than extra gifts.

Low-Cost Celebration Ideas
- Organize a cookie swap instead of buying gifts for a large group.
- Share time or skills, such as babysitting, cooking, or helping with projects.
- Create homemade gift vouchers for experiences like a family hike or a movie night at home.

Reflection Prompt
Think about last year's holiday spending. Which purchases felt meaningful, and which felt wasteful? What would you like to change this year?

The 12 Days of Minimalist Christmas

Financial mindfulness is not about being stingy. It is about spending with purpose, giving from the heart, and entering the new year with peace instead of worry.

Chapter 10
Day 10 – Acts of Kindness and Community

The holiday season is often portrayed as a time of receiving, yet some of the most meaningful moments come from giving. Not just gifts wrapped in paper, but time, attention, and care offered to others. Acts of kindness shift the focus away from consumerism and place it back on connection and compassion.

A minimalist Christmas reminds us that generosity does not have to cost much. A kind word, a shared meal, or a helping hand can matter far more than an expensive present.

Why Acts of Kindness Matter

When we serve others, we step outside our own busyness and worries. We see that the true spirit of Christmas is found in caring for one another. Kindness strengthens community, lifts spirits, and reminds us what really matters.

Key Idea: *The greatest gifts are often the ones that cannot be wrapped.*

The 12 Days of Minimalist Christmas

By practicing generosity in simple ways, we experience deeper joy ourselves while spreading light to others.

Ways to Practice Holiday Kindness

1 Give your time
Volunteer at a food bank, shelter, or community event.

2 Offer personal support
Visit an elderly neighbor, write a thoughtful card, or call someone who may be lonely.

3 Share resources
Donate clothes, toys, or books you no longer need.

4 Acts of everyday kindness
Hold the door, let someone go ahead in line, or bring a warm drink to a co-worker.

5 Involve the family
Make kindness a tradition by planning one act of service together each December.

Community Traditions to Inspire You

- Participate in a local gift drive for children or families in need.
- Organize a "kindness advent calendar" where each day highlights a small good deed.
- Join a neighborhood walk to deliver homemade cards or treats.

Reflection Prompt

Think of a time when someone showed you kindness during the holidays. How did it make you feel? How can you pass that feeling on to someone else this year?

Clara Brooks

Acts of kindness and community remind us that Christmas is not measured in money spent but in love shared. Even the smallest gesture can brighten someone's season and leave a memory that lasts long after the decorations are gone.

Chapter 11
Day 11 – Crafting Meaningful Traditions

Traditions shape the way we experience Christmas. They mark the season with familiarity and rhythm. Yet not every tradition brings joy. Some carry more stress than delight, and many continue simply because "we have always done it this way."

A minimalist approach encourages you to keep what matters and release what does not. The goal is not to strip away tradition, but to craft ones that feel meaningful, sustainable, and aligned with your values.

Why Traditions Matter

Traditions give us something to look forward to each year. They provide a sense of identity and belonging, especially for children. When chosen with care, they create lasting memories and bring people closer together.

> **Key Idea:** *The best traditions are the ones that serve you, not the ones you serve.*

By rethinking your traditions, you ensure they enrich your holiday instead of draining it.

How to Create Meaningful Traditions
1 Reflect on what matters most
Ask yourself: what do I want my family or friends to remember about Christmas?
2 Keep it simple
Choose traditions that are easy to repeat and do not require heavy planning or spending.
3 Make it personal
Focus on activities that reflect your values, culture, or personality.
4 Include experiences
Traditions built around cooking, storytelling, or shared activities are often the most memorable.
5 Be flexible
Allow traditions to evolve as life changes. A tradition should grow with you, not hold you back.

Examples of Minimalist Traditions
- Reading a special book together on Christmas Eve.
- Hosting a simple meal with close friends each December.
- Taking a yearly walk to see holiday lights.
- Practicing a "gratitude circle" where each person shares what they are thankful for.
- Starting a book-exchange night inspired by Iceland's Christmas Book Flood.

Reflection Prompt
Which traditions from your past feel heavy or obligatory? Which

The 12 Days of Minimalist Christmas

ones light you up with joy? What new traditions could you create that feel true to your values?

By crafting meaningful traditions, you make Christmas your own. Instead of following a script written by society or advertisers, you create rituals that deepen connection, reflect what you love, and can be passed on with pride.

Chapter 12
Day 12 – A Mindful Christmas Day

After weeks of preparation, Christmas Day often arrives in a blur. Between gift opening, cooking, cleaning, travel, and social visits, the day can feel more like a checklist than a celebration. A mindful approach allows you to slow down, breathe, and truly enjoy the heart of the season.

Mindfulness is simply paying attention to the present moment without rushing ahead or wishing it away. When applied to Christmas, it turns ordinary moments into cherished memories.

Why Mindfulness Matters

The pace of the day can easily sweep us along until it is over. Slowing down helps us notice the joy around us. The laughter of children, the taste of a simple meal, or the warmth of being together become more vivid when we are not distracted.

> **Key Idea:** *Presence is the greatest present you can give.*

The 12 Days of Minimalist Christmas

By making space for mindfulness, Christmas Day becomes an experience to savor rather than a task to complete.

Ways to Create a Mindful Christmas Day

1 Start with gratitude

Begin the morning by reflecting on something you are thankful for before diving into gifts or tasks.

2 Limit distractions

Make certain times of the day device-free. For example, switch off phones during meals or gift opening.

3 Simplify meals and chores

Prepare food ahead where possible and accept help with clean-up. A simpler menu leaves more time to relax.

4 Pause between activities

Take small breaks for tea, a walk, or a quiet moment to rest. These pauses create calm.

5 End with reflection

In the evening, share highlights of the day with family or write them in a journal. This creates closure and appreciation.

Mindful Alternatives to Frenzy

- Instead of rushing through presents, open them slowly and let each person share their gratitude.
- Replace a noisy afternoon of errands with a family walk outdoors.
- Choose a calm ritual such as lighting candles, reading a story, or playing gentle music.

Reflection Prompt

What do you want to remember most about this Christmas Day? How can you structure the day so that memory is possible?

Clara Brooks

* * *

By choosing mindfulness, you transform Christmas Day from a rush of activity into a celebration of presence, gratitude, and connection. This final step ties together the journey of the 12 days, leaving you with a holiday that feels rich in meaning and light in clutter.

Chapter 13
Appendix – Minimalist Christmas Checklist

Use this list as a quick guide to keep your holiday season simple, intentional, and joyful.

Day 1 – Clear the Calendar
- ☐ Write down all commitments.
- ☐ Circle the ones that truly matter.
- ☐ Decline or delegate the rest.
- ☐ Protect open days for rest and spontaneity.

Day 2 – Declutter Décor
- ☐ Unpack all decorations.
- ☐ Keep only what is meaningful or beautiful.
- ☐ Donate or recycle extras.
- ☐ Choose a simple theme or palette.
- ☐ Limit décor to a set number of boxes.

Day 3 – Rethink Gifts
- ☐ Set gift boundaries (e.g., Four Gift Rule).
- ☐ Choose experiences, consumables, or handmade items.

- ☐ Discuss limits with family and friends.
- ☐ Focus on meaning over money.

Day 4 – Simplify Wrapping and Packaging
- ☐ Use reusable fabric or recycled paper.
- ☐ Keep a small wrapping capsule.
- ☐ Decorate with natural accents.
- ☐ Avoid glittery or non-recyclable paper.

Day 5 – Declutter Digitally
- ☐ Unsubscribe from marketing emails.
- ☐ Limit time on social media.
- ☐ Create device-free moments.
- ☐ Clean out inboxes and apps.

Day 6 – Minimalist Meal Planning
- ☐ Select only the most meaningful dishes.
- ☐ Cook realistic portions.
- ☐ Share responsibilities with guests.
- ☐ Simplify ingredients and menus.

Day 7 – A Minimalist Approach with Kids
- ☐ Limit gifts to a set number.
- ☐ Create memory-focused activities.
- ☐ Teach children about generosity.
- ☐ Repeat simple, meaningful traditions.

Day 8 – Streamline Social Obligations

The 12 Days of Minimalist Christmas

- ☐ Prioritize the most meaningful gatherings.
- ☐ Decline extra invitations kindly.
- ☐ Host simply or not at all.
- ☐ Combine activities where possible.

Day 9 – Financial Mindfulness

- ☐ Set a holiday budget early.
- ☐ Track every purchase.
- ☐ Agree on limits with loved ones.
- ☐ Choose low-cost celebrations.

Day 10 – Acts of Kindness and Community

- ☐ Plan at least one act of service.
- ☐ Donate items you no longer need.
- ☐ Write cards or call someone lonely.
- ☐ Involve the family in giving.

Day 11 – Craft Meaningful Traditions

- ☐ Reflect on which traditions bring joy.
- ☐ Release heavy or stressful ones.
- ☐ Create simple, personal rituals.
- ☐ Keep traditions flexible and easy.

Day 12 – A Mindful Christmas Day

- ☐ Begin the day with gratitude.
- ☐ Create device-free times.
- ☐ Keep meals and chores simple.
- ☐ Pause often and reflect in the evening.

. . .

Reminder for the Year Ahead

Minimalism is not about removing joy. It is about creating space for joy to grow.

Conclusion – Carrying Minimalism Forward

As the decorations come down and the new year begins, it is easy to slip back into old habits. The work of a minimalist Christmas does not end on December 25. It continues in the choices you make each day about how you spend your time, money, and energy.

The past twelve days have been about more than simplifying the holidays. They have been about rediscovering what matters most. Less clutter. More connection. Fewer obligations. More joy.

What You Have Gained

By clearing your calendar, you created space for rest.

By simplifying décor, you reduced stress and waste.

By rethinking gifts, you chose meaning over obligation.

By focusing on food, traditions, and presence, you reclaimed the heart of Christmas.

> **Key Idea:** *Minimalism is not about what you remove. It is about what you make room for.*

Conclusion – Carrying Minimalism Forward

The changes may seem small, but together they build a season that feels lighter and more fulfilling.

Carrying It Into the New Year

Minimalist practices are not limited to December. The same principles can guide your daily life.
- Choose experiences over possessions.
- Protect time for rest and reflection.
- Spend money with intention.
- Keep clutter from reentering your home.
- Focus on gratitude and connection in every season.

Your Ongoing Journey

There is no single right way to live minimally. The goal is not perfection, but awareness. Each choice you make is an opportunity to align your life more closely with your values.

As you move forward, remember that simplicity is a gift you give yourself and those around you. It creates space for laughter, creativity, generosity, and peace.

Final Reflection Prompt

What lessons from this Christmas do you want to carry with you throughout the year? Write them down, and return to them when life begins to feel crowded again.

Minimalism is not the end of celebration. It is the rediscovery of joy in its purest form. As you carry these practices into the months ahead, may each season bring you clarity, connection, and the quiet confidence that less really is more.

Author's Note

When I began exploring minimalism, I never imagined how much it would reshape my holidays. Like many people, I used to measure Christmas by how much I could fit under the tree, how many parties I attended, or how perfectly decorated my home appeared. Each year I worked harder, spent more, and ended up feeling less joy.

Minimalism changed that for me. By letting go of excess, I discovered space for the things that matter most — peace, connection, gratitude, and presence. The holidays became less about performing and more about experiencing.

This book was written to share that journey. It is not a set of rigid rules, but an invitation. An invitation to slow down, to reflect, and to create a Christmas that feels rich in meaning without being weighed down by clutter or pressure.

As you read, I encourage you to adapt each idea to your own life. Keep what resonates, set aside what does not, and trust yourself to shape a season that reflects your values. Minimalism looks different for everyone, and that is what makes it powerful.

My hope is that these twelve days inspire you to rediscover the

Author's Note

quiet beauty of Christmas, to give yourself permission to rest, and to pass on traditions that nourish rather than drain.

Thank you for allowing me to walk alongside you in this season. May your holidays be lighter, brighter, and filled with the kind of joy that lasts.

With gratitude,

Clara Brooks

www.ingramcontent.com/pod-product-compliance
Lightning Source LLC
Chambersburg PA
CBHW061741070526
44585CB00024B/2771